The Sharp Edges of Water

"Come to me now once again and release me
from grueling anxiety.
All that my heart longs for,
fulfill. And be yourself my ally in love's battle."

    Sappho, translated by Julia Dubnoff

ALSO BY ANGÉLIQUE JAMAIL

Finis.

The Sharp Edges of Water

Angélique Jamail

Odeon Press

This collection contains poems that contain elements of fiction, drawn from the author's imagination and not necessarily to be construed as real.

The Sharp Edges of Water. Copyright 2018 by Angélique Jamail. All rights reserved. Produced in the United States of America.

No part of this book may be used or reproduced in any manner whatsoever without written permission of the author except in "fair use" cases of brief quotations embedded in critical articles or essays and reviews. For more information about Angélique Jamail and her work, or to contact the author, please visit her websites.

www.SapphosTorque.com
www.AngeliqueJamail.com

Published by Odeon Press.
www.OdeonPress.com

ISBN 978-1-7328629-2-0

Edited by Sarah Cortez.
Cover design by Lucianna Chixaro Ramos.
Book formatting by Jesse Gordon.

dedicated to
Alex, Allison, Amanda, Emily, and Katherine
making their ways

Table of Contents

Foreword..13

Part One: Joyride
    Moving Out..19
    Two Cities..20
    Los Angeles..22
    Joyride..24
    Book with Forgotten Title....................................26
    Listening for Atlantis..28
    A Brief and Envious History of Particle Physics.....30
    His Ballad at Breakfast..32
    The Usual..34
    Manifest Destiny...35
    After..37
    The Awakening of Jack Brown............................41
    Inamorata...42
    Joan and the City...44

Part Two: Dancing on the Sharpest Floors
    Long-Distance..49
    The Hummingbirds Warned.................................50
    Half-Truths Inside Villanelle................................51
    Bleeding the Sky...52
    Good-Night...54
    New Love in Dead Cornfields...............................55
    Cleaning House...57
    Reflection..58

Barefoot on Marble Fragments....................................59
Ruby / Renew / Redux...61

Part Three: Those Who Hold Each Other
Plan B..65
Upon Taking My Kids to the Last Roller Rink
Left in Houston..66
Summer Night Rite...67
Lullaby for a Crying Child..69
The Wilderness of Waters...70
Moving to Your Home..71
Journey..73
Commonly Occurring in Villages, in Hamlets,
and on Hearths Around Our Great Land.................74
Wedding List Poem..76
Floodtide: My Unhiding...79
The Modern Woman's Guide to Modern Life..........81
The Path Often Traveled, the Path Less
Celebrated, the Path of Ennobled Resistance
(A Rule-Breaking Poem for a Nail-Biting Vigil).....83
Letter to My Child / Self..84

Author's Note..85
Other Notes..89
Acknowledgements...91
Previously Published Poems...93
Index of First Lines..99
Ways to Support Authors...101
About the Author...103

Foreword

This is not a book of a young woman's poems nor is it the book of an elder already at peace with the quandaries and inexplicable mysteries brought by life. Instead, it bridges these two distinct ecosystems of existence by giving us the soaring richness of youthful impetuosity freighted by the middle of life's re-evaluations, honest nostalgia and regret, and a guarded hope for the future.

Given that the poet's journey has already brought both loss and hope's fracture, the poems are constructed vessels for many types of loss: the lingering heartache for a past lover; the quiet yet intrusive mourning for an adopted or abandoned city; the intermittent appraisal of a city where one grew up.

It is with Elizabeth Bishop's poem "One Art" in mind that a reader approaches and reads this volume's chronicling of loss. Bishop laid out her formal cadences to contain loss. Jamail stays with a poetic line, mostly unembraced by formal strictures. For Jamail, loss is the fecund territory complicated by the travails of geographic movement, emotional upheaval, and cultural dissonance and where the poetry sings its best. Many of these poems occur on the edges of the narrator's previous (or abbreviated) identities as daughter, lover, bride, or mother. Thus, we often hear a voice of "just a girl/sliding down alien legs/toward the bottom of the sea" ("Book with Forgotten Title").

Yet, loss in these poems, as often in real life, can engender appreciation and gratitude for what once was, whether on the material plane or on that often hazy yet intense horizon called the "emotional."

The reader finds sharply detailed portraits of both Los Angeles and Houston, the city called by the poet "my own native landscape" ("Two Cities"). The poet has built her own unique nomenclature of description for these disparate cities while honoring their individualistic natures, infamous waterways and infrastructure, vegetation and world views. Because Houston is seen through the eyes of the poet, now returned from L.A., and L.A. is seen through the same eyes of someone who both dreamed, one day, of living there yet also returned from living there, the visions of these cities become informed and satisfying. This is not a first response, nor even a second (one guesses), but a measured and nuanced response that has been years in the making with its delicious imagery and ardent longing. The pay-off for the reader lies in the unfolding of the text and sub-text as the roughly chronological poems wend the reader through the poet's movement from city to city. Another poet-chronicler of Los Angeles is Luis J. Rodriguez, who used anger's white-hot glare to write *The Concrete River*. Angelique Jamail's poems about the same city are cooler. They bring the faceted yearning after both hope and regret, with love played against distance and dreams, which are strategically balanced by "the sheer drop-off on the other side of the road" ("Joyride").

I would like to point the reader to yet another treasure contained in the book: the use of water's many forms. Moisture, dew, fog, tears, oceans, bayous, rain, flood, ice, snow—they are all in the poems. Perhaps, it should not be surprising that a book containing such powerful instances of loss would also contain so many instances of homage to the most illustrative and evocative symbol of the unconscious: water. All these manifestations of content through water's imagery rise (or fall) unbidden, magical, perfect in context. Our poet is willing to dive deep in her poems and takes us with her.

I encourage you to "jump into the wet sky" ("Moving to Your Home") with the poet. Don't hesitate. She won't lose you. And you'll enjoy the swim inside the sharp edges of water.

Sarah Cortez
Houston, Texas

Part One:
Joyride

Moving Out

my room
                         old and cracked

these walls
                         cinder-block

this paint
                         cracked and peeling

memories
                         forced through a dark canal

their hands
                         tug and pull

unwilling recall
                         jump and bounce
                         hurtle and fall

crowded old room

Two Cities

I.

O Los Angeles, your grumbling
tumbling shivers and quakes
go half-unnoticed most of the time,
the evidence of which we know
when we get home from work to find
a curio fallen off a shelf, a terra
cotta figure the cat stalked over
to kick around with its barely
interested paw.

II.

My own native landscape:
a flat transgression of static lack
of terrain, the washed-down, worn-
out concrete parks and parking lots
and permits nine ways to Sunday
to save the oldest trees in a gentrifying
neighborhood, and how many ways
can I explain it to someone who has never
known this wet heat and muddy
water and map of the city's
bayous that looks like bleu cheese?

Los Angeles

Los Angeles isn't flat
like Houston, where I'm from.
It has curves and slopes, *terrain*.
When I look off a freeway overpass
in Los Angeles, I see dynamic miles,
miniature forests between
concrete and stucco neighborhoods,
covens of disinhibition,
a nudist colony.

Even from the observation deck of an office
building back home, looking down on the city
shows me treetops like so much broccoli,
flat industrial park roofs,
a few congested streets.

But buildings of the L.A. skyline
pierce the layer-cake smog
of brown, gray, purple air
that makes you choke and
gives the sunset its Easter-echo colors.

Beyond the skyline are *mountains*,
megaliths hazy in jellyfish air,
hulking cloudbanks of deep lavender
blending into the sky strata,
the skyline against their shadows
like needles in a pincushion
set against the ghosts of rocks
slowly fading even before we arrived.

I watch from the overpass
as the hills turn and twist,
those hills that are the freeway,
the freeway like mine back home,
the only hills I have.

Joyride

The engine cries
like a nest of hungry kittens
as the needle passes ninety

Drops come in
from the crack in the window

Your mind,
blank,
just a dark cloud
flashes of memory interrupting
like some bitter song
that won't stop ringing
in your ears until you focus
on the outer fringes—

Pounding thunder,
rain pelting sheets, water
coating the windshield,
wipers barely working—

You're hugging the curves
of this mountain road
as they call to you
like friends in the dark,
but you're afraid to answer

You can't see ahead of you
but it doesn't matter now

All that is left:
you,
the mountain,
the thunder and the rain,
and the sheer drop-off on the other side of the road

Book with Forgotten Title

I remember a princess
    flowing hair wet dress
trapped by an ogre
    overfull
      welcome to my cave
jars on shelves hold souls
    his collection under the foam
he keeps her waiting
    whole

she might not have been a princess
    but just a girl
sliding down alien legs
toward the bottom of the sea
stalks cut off
    kelp empty
below the knees and
a disappearance into nothing

headfirst slow descent
through tangled water
    unsure of what is but she
    feels it green and blue and purple
she screams
listens to her voice
    undulate
        down and back and
    bellow up to meet her
bump around the strips of kelp
like long wanderings of ripped silk
    hung in a breeze
        and the voice eases her down

when she finds the end
will those alien legs jump
and carry her away
      to the cave of the soul
           keeper—

I don't know yet
I don't know yet

Listening for Atlantis

Down this deep, debate over waves
and particles can be settled.

The light, granular, spotted
by sand I've disturbed, has sunk

too far to be tossed by rip currents above,
and the fringe of my hair

trickles like midnight behind me.
Salt stings grit against my skin.

Down here? More than quiet:
even the dense cold can't coax

my ears into soundful vessels,
leaves me the narrow trench of silence.

Finding the roil of my own voice
won't climb this steep, smooth slope

any more than I can grind pearls
to spice under my bare feet.

In the foam-green light,
a seahorse, reluctant, divines his way

toward me, his every watery breath
an inconsequential sponge, squeezed.

The silent currents hide dunes, a city,
an ecology of the mystical and mundane;

still I leap across the sand, a –naut,
an eddy, a pilgrim in the deepening dusk of loss.

A Brief and Envious History of Particle Physics
Los Angeles, California

O painted, sun-glinting
mecca, every large, flat,
vertical surface calls out
to me with singular insistence.

Den of airbrushed self-
consciousness, studied
perfection, your charmed
denizens are real, real,

real enough. I am
torn into particular
fragments. I adore
your graceful hills, your

mountains like jauntily
sculpted mounds rising
from the sleepy curves
of the world, your determined

blue sky, your laughable clouds,
your cold ocean sucking at
the hot sandy edge
of the land, your palm

trees stuck up from the ground
like frilled toothpicks,
your all-night pizza
delivery diners, your recklessly

entranced tourists, your warm
expatriate Texans migrated
west, staring in secret wonder
at the generosity of your openness.

I miss you, other home,
landscape of my heart
and welcoming witness to
my strange quirks.

I miss the self I was when
you were mine, I miss the parts
of me left languishing
in the settles of your valleys.

From the top stratum
of violet air above the
hills to the bottom of
every car-studded canyon,

I could give up
each grain of pretense,
and spiral down into your
exquisite, sloping life.

His Ballad at Breakfast

I see you, my gray wool sweater
shrugs off my shoulders, falls
to the floor, shatters on the cold
marble like ice.

I watch your hair dry from across
the breakfast table each
morning (fresh from the shower,
your ears like washed peaches)

over toast and marmalade and
juice, the steam of the tea —
its mist rises into the air,
a quiet effacing.

Ice-heavy trees hang over the fence;
we watch wind through the window
pull glass branches to the ground.
The stove's heat is weak.

You offer to go out for wood,
but I would rather you not
leave me. I touch your hand to make
sure you are still solid,

not vanishing, when I turn back
from the pantry. We go back
to bed. I lie close to watch
your sleeping breath; I do

not want to sleep. I wonder if
you'll have to leave. You turn
to the wall in your sleep, taking
the wool blanket with you.

The Usual

In your room with the fireplace, still
                              I waited.

The long-unused room smelled of summer heat—
and of hate, too, but not mine.
Every tick of the clock, a bullet
exploding—blasting away the empty space
in the room with no furniture but dust
on the floor—till you arrived. The door
opened and you stood, eyes like cracked glass.

When you spoke I knew you were lying.
I could see shrapnel of the truth flying
away unchecked, stuck in the air to your words—
a different cast from the words I'd just heard
you say. The tedium dragged and you
kept telling me stories, making more excuses.

Fifty-five fingers couldn't stop the killing time,
and on your lips they couldn't have stopped your lies.

Manifest Destiny
West on Interstate-10

The long and lonely road stretches
before me with a sense of peace,
a finality that prompts me
to sit and let the moments pass
away unchecked... Mutely I stare
at the short white dashes of time

as they slip past in perfect time
with the wheels as they course the stretch
of highway... My eyes stare
but see only the calm, the peace
of a lack of life on the sterile pass,
a strange place that scares me...

I left, nothing to anchor me
to that gray place where only time
makes any progress... A car passes,
fades quickly behind me... Now I stretch
my neck to witness the cold peace
that car knows, receding down the road... I stare

at my reflection, but don't stare
at that car's image leaving my
mirrored view... I embrace quiet, peace,
as one by one the dashes of time
fly past me, their bodies stretching
to cover the highway... The sun passes

the hills on the edge of the pass. . .
Heedless of the brightness I stare
at the orange and red light stretching
across the sky. . . The sun warms my
body and car, making the time
fade more slowly in this strange peace. . .

How much more of this eerie peace
can I stand? On the endless pass
the car accelerates, the time
goes even more slowly. . . I stare
at the mocking clock on my
dashboard. . . The minutes are stretching

into oblivion. . . I stare
and let pass the dashes of time. . .
Mind-numbing, endless, this peaceful stretch. . .

After

I. Loss

He remembers her hair,
the way it used to stare
at him over toast and
juice, drying the morning.
Her skin, soft as warm sand
with no shells, drank the steam
of the ginger tea
she preferred to coffee.

When she left he couldn't
eat. Juice and toast didn't
taste the same. He spent two
hours glaring at maps. She
was driving to the coast, two
days in a car, kept company
by boxes piled to the windows.

He thinks about the way she walked the first
day he met her. He fumbles for a scrap
of paper—a poem he wrote for her: "She
was pretty / unselfconscious / unable
to be kept / from doing anything / she
wanted—" But he'd never finished it. He
wanted never to be done with her.

II. Mapping

At first there was the drive.
It stretched, endless. Her mind
was numb. She had brief thoughts
of turning back, saying
quietly she'd been wrong,
going back to the place
she knew: her family, the
old house. . . But it was he

who convinced her to stay
on that road the first day:
she assumed he'd wait for
her, in the same way he
had done. So she took more
time, more space, more highway.
She felt the miles pass,
counting their weight, adding

to what lay before her on the droning
stretch of highway, what waited for her on
the coast, beyond the desert and mountains,
past plains and every new terrain,
where she would meet herself in the new place
for the first time, talking to new people,
dancing on new floors, trying.

III. Jealously

He moves slowly through the
house, listening for her
voice he knows will not speak
to him today, not here.
He knows that she will speak
to someone else, somewhere
on the coast. And he knows
he won't hear her feet

stepping quietly on
the hardwood floors in
the dark house, but somewhere else
she dances and she walks,
she listens to the bells
of some other church, talks
to other people in
another place. He thinks

he might go insane if he does not
get out of the house. He puts on his sweater,
that she gave him when she left the first
time, and goes out into the cold gray air.
Ice-heavy trees hang low over fences,
and cars blanketed in strange glass-marble
make him cold, but he's not inside. And not waiting.

IV. Her Own

She is pretty
unselfconscious
unable to be kept
She does anything
She wants—

The Awakening of Jack Brown

His was one firm hand that grabbed at nothing
as she was pulled through the wound in the wall
where the dog had broken through it.

Her hand at the end of the leash jolted forward,
and she slipped through the opening arm-first,

then the mongrel dragged her twisting figure
through the next aspect of the world.

He stared in troubled curiosity at the woman departing,
and at his dog pulling her away.

Inamorata

I cannot tell you
why I cannot love you
using such stinging words.
I cannot love you
lacerates the roof of
my mouth, scalds my
tongue. Instead I
use beautiful words, ugly
as broken brown eggshells
in your heart:
shiksa,
    Arab,
        Texan.

Why must everything resolve
down to faith and distance?
It was the same with my
father. It is not enough
that I have faith, not enough that
I am not distant. And this I
cannot unlearn, any more
than I can love you,
so far away from
where and what I am.

I would live in the press
of your hands on the small
of my back, live in the warm
breath of my lips under your
ear. I would count every
step you walked away from
me like possessions taken

from my house, and when
you smiled, another piece
of furniture would come
back. See, there's a chair, and
there a desk. If you sat down to
eat with me, my bed would waltz
through the front door and pass
us on its way down the hall. But
then I would diminish in a flurry
of missals, for I cannot
love you.

Joan and the City

She stood, chained to
a pole, in a sackcloth dress.

> *The fire was my Pentecost.*

Anno Domini 1431:
She heard those same Voices,
from the throats of God and Angels,
in the sizzle of her sweat
on the wood.

St. Michael spoke
to her as the flames

> *purified the sins of*
> *the court in*
> *my sacrifice:*

crisped her toenails.

The Voices were present
the day she was killed
for her heresies: putting on the
pants of a man, taking up
a sword in the service of King
Charles of France—

> *in the service of God—*

claiming Divine influence.

*The fire was the Holy Ghost
bringing me back to God.*

Anno Domini 1455:
She will be retried,
a pile of ash on the stand,
magistrates screaming at its charred
softness to speak truth.

    The ash will say nothing,

just as helpful as a girl
torn from truth from safety from promises
but never from belief.

Part Two:
Dancing on the Sharpest Floors

Long-Distance

midnight here, two in the
morning your time

I feel you sleeping: a
little part of me has

numbed, as if
lost coherence, as if

two hours ahead of
the rest of me, as if

heavy slow breathing,
waiting for the rest

catch up
slow down

The Hummingbirds Warned

Ten hummingbirds sat buzzing, hovering
in the haze over a telephone wire,
until one by one the prickling plummeted
them like secrets zapped to the ground, their fall
a betrayal by the very apparatus
which, formerly, had made their little wings
beat with such dizzying speed.

Half-Truths Inside Villanelle

There was no expression in his eyes
when he said her affectionate nature caused him pain.
These were things she had never realized.

She'd never thought of touching hair and arms and
    thighs
and lips as sacred, as not being the same as a friend's
    embrace.
With no expression in his eyes

he said, quietly, that he would apprise
her of the difficult faithfulness of love — he made it plain,
but it was something she had never realized.

He offered, for her instruction, to stare into the eyes
of some girl they both knew. He said —
and there was a quick expression in his eyes

when he said it — that she would cry
to see him smiling, whispering in that ear one day.
This was something she had never realized.

She understands him now when she thinks of the lies
he must have thought she said.
There is no expression in his eyes.
These were things she had never realized.

Bleeding the Sky

In the time when my fingernails
were painted with a color
called "Granite," I wished
for a marvel as poetic as the sky's and knew—as do sage
gods—it did not exist, could not
exist, as long as I thought about it, hoped for it.

I understood finally that it
was no small thing if I dragged my fingernails
across the sky, drastic as a blackboard in knots.
It would bleed with a bold color,
hues of wild primrose and sage
bound with the strings of a deep red wish.

And I read other poems, wishes
of people who could scrape beyond this
perfection, past the sky where stars lay like sage
old nuns, granite pebbles, breaking my thin fingernails
when I argued and tried to write their pale colors
out of the sky. And those other poems were not

gentle! Their words twisted my heart into knots
and turned my brain onto its side, wishing
for darkness to overpower their colors:
fear and passion and shame and anger, and love
   so deep it
grows outward from myself until its reach is longer
   than my fingertips
even after I've stretched my arms out to touch the
   sagging

sky. And those other words *were* the sky, painted in
    colors of sage
and wild primrose and granite and black and red,
    a love-knot
unforgiving of my fumbling fingers.
But I wanted to write! And even so I wished
a paradox: for you to hold my impulse down, to keep it
from spilling the perfect sky's blood-colors

on my hands. But even now I can't keep the colors
from their heaviness, stop them from sagging.
Had you been there you'd have had no small task
    holding it,
that fire-out-of-bounds impulse, and I could not
have been responsible for my actions or my wishes…
Still, I might have saved that expanse from my nails

by the exquisite distraction of you, my fingers dipped
    in colors
of sage and wild primrose red, hues of wishes
never before filled, unashamed to paint granite words
    all over you and love it.

Good-Night

small sweet pieces of time crumbling away
the craving echo underneath the static hum
your hair dangled over my gasp

on the pale pistachio wall upstairs
a cracking clockface helped him wait for you

gray silence dropping underneath the sink
into the still pool of questions collected there

where you give a scratched response

clouds—their sharp gray edges pencil-
drawn against a dark blue page, the canvas sky

their billows, bulbous bones thrown
into a yard where birds dart under airplanes

the machine-drone noise across your ears
was his voice lecturing against the sky

New Love in Dead Cornfields

Memories quicken my pulse
when I think of how we strode
through the funhouse of artists and thinkers
that year the corn didn't grow.
They beat out rain-dances on the walls
with paintbrushes, charcoal, and empty-paged books
while we marched past each closed door
and every muffled prayer. The mirrors
were hung with towels as if death
had taken everyone by surprise, and even
the writers couldn't figure out how to cope
with this dry spell.

I felt old and familiar when you led me
out the back door and onto the rows of plowed dirt.
The tall joys of sitting cross-legged
in those hesitant, sown fields of fecund not-yets
were our thrown-to-the-sun discoveries,
the most ineffectual revelations
on a most ineffectual harvest.
We made a gift of feeling
in this pursuit of strained giving,
begging the ground for food
and from each other, our stare-eyed patience.

The craze of collecting surprises,
one kernel in each pocket and a
love-letter in your shirt,
started to involve the very dirt and sky,
and the haunting, used principles
of withholding, withdrawing, and retreat
shrieked and screamed the wild west of our planting
until I said, *No more,* and it was back,
back, back to the east, and your tender verve died, too.

Cleaning House

I wash your letters
in the kitchen sink
until the ink fades
and your lies swirl
down the drain.
You have left me
blank as eggshells.

I will crisp pictures
of you like bacon
in the pan, my greasy
memories the molten fat
that I will pour down
the kitchen sink.

The lack of my life
in your life sludges
over me and hardens.
I wash my memories
of you with the rest
of the laundry, tangled
and pulled apart, tangled
and pulled apart, tangled
and pulled. Apart.

Reflection

in a throbbing fog, I walk the hall
aching, my limbs heavy
wading through phantom water

Barefoot on Marble Fragments

languish under dust like the palest sheets
on every wall and table in the house

wait for clouds to drip and drizzle so you
can say you knew it would rain

stare by the easel near the window
at the free, determined traffic of people living

> *my brave bare feet*

greenness eroded like beachhead
under the weight of scorn and time

> *recognition that pierces*
> *the limping comfort of the norm*

settle, claw your way toward the first secure-
seeming thing in your path and never peer beyond

> *while I dance shoeless on the sharpest floors*
> *tossing pieces of myself*
> *into the air, realizing they might not be*
> *caught*

we must plant the things we love in so many places
they can never be lost

> *a light-stepped waltz across broken-edged marble*

dance on the blood-feet again
or never walk

Ruby / Renew / Redux

There was fear
fear of the light fear of the dark
fear you would leave fear you would stay
fear of your greedy wolf growl
I was a red-hooded wreck

But I folded my fear
into a tight bundle and burnt
it into a loaf of bread
and fed it to you

You devoured the whole
felt queasy after dinner
cold sweat and a stone in your stomach

Part Three:
Those Who Hold Each Other

Plan B

Golden ball like a prophet,
predict for the princess her fate:
>   a frog lapping wine from her cup,
>   digesting the food from her plate,
>   his eager tongue tickling her belly,
>   his sticky feet crawling along her—
>   then in the morning a man in her bed
>   and a quick-arranged marriage by Father.

Golden ball, keep your playmate:
warn her not to whine for help,
but to keep her freedom for longer
by fetching you for herself.

Upon Taking My Kids to the Last Roller Rink Left in Houston

I was a roller skating queen
when I was twelve. I knew all
the rinks of this town like a master
harper knows the pluck
and tang of every singing string.

Now, at a mortal forty-four, one
busted tailbone in my past, my wheels
feel every scratch and patch
of this decades-old floor, every
whoosh of every godlike adolescent
zooming by.
         My hair blown back
by the breeze of my own perched
recklessness, I wish I had the brass ball
bearings for roller derby.

Summer Night Rite
Houston, Texas

lizards crawl all over
our house, pale velvet greens
against a humid gray stucco turned
silver by the streetlamp

soundtrack of the night's moist creatures
air smells of wet mulch
and the soaked heaviness of the season

we drive in almost-rain,
waiting for water to come
      having teased us all day
      stickying our skin and thickening
      each strand of our almost-curly hair
restless from the weight
of a whole day's almost-accomplishments

we hope the rains breathe
a cool lift into our sleep

soon, the usual torrent

houses dig their heels into ditches
across from the freeway embankment

the leaves in the street
in our headlights are frogs staring
up, water falling on mottled faces

droplets slide down the curves
of the car, of the streetlamp, and of
the lizards as we park and drift inside

we drip our way upstairs and leave puddles
of clothes on the bathroom floor

the stillness exhales;
bathed in sky, we sleep

Lullaby for a Crying Child

When my cousin died, olive skin and thick
    black hair and twelve years old laid under
        dirt and roses, I found out death's simple

trick: it's no one-way gate, but a long silk
    skirt in the rain. I peel the silk from my
        skin, hang it dripping in the bathroom.

My cousin defies death's veil, ages beyond his
    allotted years, finds me in a dream, touches
        my hands. I look at him, through him, and

wake to rain. Left but not alone. My skirt
    dripping on the tile.

The Wilderness of Waters

Your ocean here is warm and green.
I'm trying to get used to it,
but I still miss my cold, gray sea.

Such warm waters as I've never been
in, such strange creatures have I met.
Your ocean here is warm and green.

Some say, "All marine is marine,"
that I should be well any wet,
but I still miss my cold, gray sea.

My chill churning sea washed me clean,
but these warm waters just make me wet.
Your ocean here is warm and green.

Finally now do you swim with me,
and so moving here is a choice-not-regret,
but I still miss my cold, gray sea.

I want to wring a life out of *this* marine,
but it may take many tides to get used to it.
Your ocean here is warm and green,
and I still miss my cold, gray sea.

Moving to Your Home

We've been sitting on the bed
in the place where it rains
every afternoon as a part
of the natural order of things.
The afternoons become evenings
quickly here under the rainy sky.

I recall an afternoon when a green sky
made me want to crawl into bed
and wait for the dark, wet evening
to clean the greenness away with rain.
The sky's light washed all of our things
in a pale green bath, and a part

of me wished we could make a departure
from this place, jump into the wet sky,
let go of my blanket-cocoon and all our things,
keeping only the memory of our bed
in a soon-to-be swallowed land. I trembled for rain
to wash the daylight out of the evening

air, but the green tint slid even
onto the darkness, partially
dripped in sheets by the rain,
partially a reflection on the sky
of the wet trees. The window by the bed
shook with the wind, and little things

started to scare me. I packed a few things
into a satchel in case we left for the evening
to sleep in your old bed
at your parents' house. They were never a part
of the plan, but even I could not resist the sky's
thundering, the ugly greenness of rain.

Now, wrapped in the blanket, we watch the rain
dripping rivers on the window. You reassure me
    our things
will be safe in this house, under this sky,
under our bed, and that we will stay home all evening.
I'm not wild about the weather here, but I guess it's part
and parcel of being with you, together in this bed,

in this house, under this rainy sky,
on an island where people leave their
    things under their beds
and the evening is part of the afternoon.

Journey

I wait behind the closed chapel doors, hanging on my father's arm as if he were the most important, most stable man I'd ever met. Schubert's "Ave Maria," plucked by a string trio in the cavernous hall on the other side of those doors, lilts its way toward me, the notes lifting the edges of my veil and sliding in and out of my hair.

"You okay, honey?" my father murmurs, smiling. I squeeze my fingers on his arm and nod, fragile as *a girl's wrist*, as the doors yawn open and three hundred people stand.

Every step down that path toward the most important, most stable man I've ever known is a step farther away from everything I no longer want to be and everything I have always been.

But finally, each step a sob, choking and gasping and trying to hold it in, I reach the end of the path, and the veil is lifted and my new life, my new self, *breaks into blossom* like a rose made of diamond bursting out of a rose made of glass.

Commonly Occurring in Villages, in Hamlets, and on Hearths Around Our Great Land

Fourteen cows piled themselves onto the New Jersey
    turnpike
last Friday afternoon in homage
to the first fair minutes of the new moon.

Traffic stopped for miles on either side
of these giant Holstein-spotted and
udder-bearing nourishers who silently

and with dignity intact walked into the middle
of the road and climbed up onto each other's backs
and closed their eyes, noses pressed

into flanks and tails swishing
tunnel-flies from their neighbors' ears
in compassionate solidarity.

Not one single low moved through the confused air,
but fourteen pairs of mindful eyes tilted
upward from behind twenty-eight

rows of silky brown lashes, as if
looking through their blinders
to the empty space in the too-bright sky,

to where the moon would have been
if it were at the other end of its cycle;
and hundreds of angry, confused, frustrated

horns tried to break the splendor
of the silent cows
who held each other and would hold each other.

Our demands will be met.

Wedding List Poem

countdown calendar of what to do and when
will the calendar fit my needs? because *I* am not typical

two-foot stack of wedding dress magazines
four-foot stack of wedding dresses on the
    fitting room floor
sketch of what I want my dress to look like
list of bridesmaids
list of things I don't want to argue about with my
    mother
list of things we don't need to do until next month

nine months to go
debate over whether to invite our friends' children
what can we afford?
list of deposits that need to be made
guest list, growing
list of things we put off until next month

six months to go
list of things I didn't realize I would argue about with
    my father
people who keep telling us to elope, as if that wouldn't
    cause a whole new list of troubles
wedding dress, maid of honor's dress, flower girl's dress
    hanging in a closet at my parents' house
stark satin reminder to watch my weight and a boned
    corset in case I don't
buying *two* veils to get *just* the right look
a patient fiancé who must not see The Dress

such nice people who want to help out
bridal shower games
five weddings this fall (one won't last the year)
guest list, still growing, minus one uncle
flowers for mourning…
flowers for the wedding, still not chosen
list of things we have put off too long

two months to go
vows to write and poems to read
list of ways to have a civil ceremony without upsetting
    too many guests
people whom I wish would just *trust* my artistic vision
being reminded that this is not about the couple getting
    married
list of ways to make concessions
magazines which foster the lie that the whole process is
    about the bride being a princess for a day
finding out the veil is a traditional symbol of feminine
    submission
being reminded again of who's paying for the wedding
list of things we pay for ourselves
guest list, still incomplete, still growing
recuperative values of each possible honeymoon venue
list of out-of-town guests we don't expect to come
list of things we have forgotten

guest list, way too long for the ballroom
guest list, cuts made to
guest list, when was the last time we went out to dinner
    with them?
guest list, counting and counting and counting until the
    numbers match the needs

six weeks to go
my fiancé laughing as I thumb through a notebook of
 lists
crazed, laughing bonfire of those damned bride
 magazines
list of little details we will have forgotten in the week
 before the wedding
(copies of that list in case we lose it)
list of ways my mom is actually making
 this beautiful for me
times I feel gratitude to my father

list of gifts, list of thank-yous
important moments, important people
photographs, songs
list of things—
 all it is, is things.

Floodtide: My Unhiding

There was a cape, cold and wet and worn, that he said had belonged to his four-times-great-uncle, a pirate-ship captain—which would, I suppose, have made that uncle a pirate and my friend a pirate four-times-removed. I should have known *that* before: when he put on that cape, the end of his belt, hanging down at his waist, became a sword.

He had been wearing the cape outside in the rain. I was cold, and so I curled up in it so my fins could stretch out, unfurl, as I day-dreamed of home, my home just off the cape.

He had never seen me in my home. He knew me only as I am when I walk; he had never seen me swim, never seen me glide through the tide undulating like the mathematical waves he understands, following the currents I understand. But I couldn't help my homesickness when I saw him, wet, walk back inside the beach house, out of the rain thundering out in the cape which is my real home, under the shelter of the cape which was his four-times-great-uncle's. He slid the fabric—heavy and salt-air water dripping steadily onto the sea-shell fossil floor—off his shoulders, and the sword evaporated. He smiled.

I tiptoed to the cape and wrapped it around my body, my long dress spreading as the water wrapped my legs together and stretched the fins back out. *I* smiled.

He looked at me, eyes surprised and mouth gaping like a trapped fish. But I was glad he knew, now, and that my awkward secret was unfolded.

I don't think he'll keep me, now, trapped inside this house, although he did it without knowing, before. He'd called it "our" beach house, and I'd always smiled and watched the waves behind my eyelids, trying not to feel the ring he'd given me and wishing I'd told him before where my home *really* was, and hadn't said just "the cape."

On his lips my name is still "Love," although his eyes dart fast away, and his hands are afraid to touch what he thinks I have become. In fact, I have always been this and only pretended otherwise, so I suppose my change has been into the truth; wrapped in the truth-cape, now I swim in the cape.

He will not swim with me, but he waits on the beach each night, holding the cape to hold me in when I, wet and cold and still strange to him, emerge from the cold water, my legs splitting from the dark sea into pale flesh, discarded scales dripping into my briny bath.

And I smile to see his wonder at my transformation, his color rising like the tide into his cheeks, but he walks back in with me, to our beach house, a refuge from the sea and the glory of my unhiding.

The Modern Woman's Guide to Modern Life

It has been made quite clear that the world
is no longer safe for fairy tales,

that women cannot flit about
the woods alone,

> We must avoid the lilting solitude
> of the forest as much as

    picking
flowers and reciting poetry
in some sun-dappled meadow,

> we must shun
> the strong men who wait for us there,

waiting for a dashing young man —*rich*—
on a beast worthy of the title *steed*,

> no matter how often our fathers
> called us "Princess" when we were children,

that we were born for something
more substantial,

> for that title now is like
> venom, sprayed from the garden

that there wasn't much wrong
with that original construct
except for its implied and
necessary catatonia,

                              sprinklers we ran through in
                      tiny polka-dot bikinis on hot days.

that life and

                          We must make our own stories,
                kiss away the witches' evil reputations,
            bite down hard on every deep red apple

           the fevered pursuit
of it

        because despite the warnings to the contrary,

    are yet too much with us.

                it does in fact taste pretty good.

The Path Often Traveled, the Path Less Celebrated, the Path of Ennobled Resistance (A Rule-Breaking Poem for a Nail-Biting Vigil)

Do not go gentle into that stifling night;
Rage, rage against the snuffing of the light.

Do not go gentle into those good old days which
    were truly night;
Rage, rage against the smothering of the light.

Do not go gentle into that locker room of night;
Rage, rage against the rape of the light.

Do not go gentle into that back alley of the night;
Rage, rage against the beat-down of the light.

Do not go gentle into that Burning Time of night;
Rage, rage against the murder of the light.

Do not go gentle into that murderous night;
Rage, rage against the silencing of the light.

Do not go gentle into that good old boys' night;
Rage, rage against the extermination of the light.

Crash ungently into that glass sky, crash into the night,
and be light.

Letter to My Child / Self

Little bird
your body feels hollow now
but living in the world
will fill you up

will make your bones hard
strong as steel beams
to stretch your delicate
skin across

to cage inside
your bruised heart
clenched belly
and all the nourishing
venom you'll ever
need.

Author's Note

There is something to be said for publishing early in your writing career, and something else entirely to be said for waiting.

The first book of mine ever to see the light of day was a chapbook of poetry entitled *Gypsies*, a title I would never have chosen in this somewhat more enlightened time. It was essentially my Senior Honors Thesis when I finished my degree in Creative Writing from The University of Houston, and while I was proud of it at the time, I was also twenty-three and maybe an idiot.

The chapbook was, for me, a tangible representation of the extremely hard work I had done to learn not just how to write, but also to love, poetry. I had entered UH as a fiction student and was graduating as a poet. My love of storytelling and lifelong desire to be a novelist were satisfied only slightly by a file of unpublished short stories in my desk, a small notebook with the opening chapters of my first novel (a high fantasy which ran aground in chapter six and has never yet made its way back out to sea), and the loosely strung narrative I'd crafted out of the poems I'd written during my last two years of college. That tenuously narrative collection was my chapbook, and it sold about five hundred copies, and if any of you still has one of those, let me know. I'll trade you for it with something else that's better.

My second chapbook, *Barefoot on Marble*, came out

several years later to similar fanfare. I am definitely *not* ungrateful for the support and enthusiasm it received, but I didn't complain when it went out of print, either.

Flash forward to my thirties and the beginning of my far better life, when I had a young family and had returned to writing fiction. I can't say I had much in the way of regrets regarding my writing career, except that I wished I had more work out in the world. Remember how I said that in college I needed to learn how to love poetry? That's true. I hadn't read much of it growing up beyond what was thrust at me in school. And while I maintain that I had extraordinarily good English teachers throughout most of high school (I'm looking at you, Mrs. Pierce, Mrs. Wilson, and Mr. Novo), I can't say that we ever spent much time reading poetry that I enjoyed. We read a few of the war poets of World War I and the best-known poems of Robert Frost. Some of the edgier girls in my class read Sylvia Plath on the sly. In ninth grade we conquered a whole page out of *The Odyssey* (the episode of the lotos eaters, which—taken out of context—freaked me out). I accidentally found my way to Sara Teasdale (via a short story by Ray Bradbury) and Edna St. Vincent Millay (via speech and debate) and camped out in their parlors. I legitimately adored Shakespeare.

But a foundational love of poetry this sampling does not make.

Eventually I came to love poetry because my professors at UH made me write it. In form, usually. And then to read it, the recent stuff, the stuff that was being written by poets who were still alive. Contemporary poetry found its way into my life, and at first I didn't even balk at the label "confessional." I didn't yet know enough about the world to recognize the problems with that. I also didn't know yet that the poetry of women's experience would be less valued in the literary world than men's, for reasons that both still elude me and don't.

We have traveled a long way since then, made it clear into another century and figured a few things out. And my work, too, has evolved, branched out in many directions. I am most definitely both a poet and a fiction writer now. What I had to learn about language after writing nothing but poetry for a number of years made my prose better. And what I came to understand about story and the human condition from writing fiction has made my poetry more worthwhile.

In between the publication of those two chapbooks and *The Sharp Edges of Water* have been many manuscripts in many genres, some of them even published or in the queue now. But what I love about this book, the one you're holding in your hands, is that it is not so much about me, but about many parts of me and many pieces of the world and many parts of my experiences and many parts of my early writing career. When I handed the first completed draft of it to my editor, Sarah Cortez, there were fifty poems in there, poems I had written over the course of my adult life thus far. Some of them came from *Gypsies* and *Barefoot on Marble* but had been rewritten in my grown-up voice, sometimes drastically altered to be almost unrecognizable. Some of the poems were brand-new and written just weeks before I turned the manuscript in. The rest were a mix of the years in between, when I had been writing fiction but kept pulling back to poetry for one reason or another. Sarah took those fifty poems and, using her gift of insight, culled them down to just what you have here, chiseling a fascinating narrative out of them that I love.

I hope you enjoy this book of poems, this book of stories, and that wherever you are in your life you open yourself up to the immensity of perception. Get beyond the screens that seem to want to trap us into a world only a few inches wide, and make poems out of life, and make stories out of poetry. And then write them down. You'll probably love what that does for you.

Angélique Jamail
Houston, Texas
October 2018

Other Notes

"Book with Forgotten Title" is an ekphrastic poem inspired by *Black* from *Brushstrokes in Different Colors in Two Directions* (1993) by Sol LeWitt.

The italicized phrases in the prose-poem "Journey" are quoted or paraphrased from the poem "A Blessing" by James Wright.

The epigraph to this book is from Julia Dubnoff's translation of Sappho's "Prayer to Aphrodite" and is used with permission from the translator and from Harvard's Center for Hellenic Studies, for whom the translation was initially done. For more information, please see chs.harvard.edu/publications.

Acknowledgements

This book and this author owe a debt of gratitude to many people, and I'm going to try here and make sure to include everyone.

Thank you to Sarah Cortez, my editor, whose insight has been invaluable.

Thank you to Christa Forster, who pointed me toward Sarah C. in the first place and who also provided me with deeply helpful beta reading and critiques.

Thank you to my brother Myles Jamail, for sensitivity reading on some of my work and for general support and love.

Thank you to Sarah Warburton and David Jón Fuller, cherished writing friends who not only keep me honest about writing fiction but who also are really good at talking me down off the Writer Brain™ ledge.

Thank you to Melissa Huckabay for cathartic Saturday morning writing dates at Panera as often as we can manage it.

Thank you to Babette Hale, Adam Holt, Brenda Leibling-Goldberg, Meredith Moore, Shirley Redwine, Lucie Scott-Smith, and Jenny Waldo for being such an excellent critique group over the years. Thanks also to Adam for guiding me through the Kickstarter process and convincing me I could do it, and to Jenny for valuable insight from her own experience.

Thank you to Jesse Gordon, the best book designer ever, and Lucianna Chixaro Ramos, an amazing and patient cover designer and artist.

Thank you to Rick Lupert for the blurb and for keeping the Los Angeles poetry scene alive in my heart and memory and for giving me the opportunity to read my work out there when I was borrowing his city for a while.

Thank you to my students, who inspire me to do better all the time.

Thank you to the amazing and generous people who supported the Kickstarter for this book; I am humbled by how fortunate you've made me feel. In particular, thank you to Libby Ingrassia Bergman, Katie Brass, Cindy Clayton, Viviana Denechaud, Larry Eshleman, John Hovig, Josh Hudley, Chuck Ivy, Mona Miles, Marcie Newton, Amber Reed and Justin Jamail, Kevin Roberts-Roppa, Jennifer Sanders, Justin Segal, and Lauren Volness.

Thank you also, so very much, to my family, including my parents Robby and Monetta Jamail and my brother Robert Jamail for their love and support, and most especially to Aaron, Hannah, and Liam, without whose encouragement and patience and trust in a positive outcome and in a purpose to my work I couldn't possibly manage to be an author or even, maybe, a writer.

And of course, thank you to my readers. Yes, I do this whole writing thing for me, but if I'm being honest, I also really, really, really do it for you.

Thank you thank you thank you thank you thank you.

Previously Published Poems

Some of the poems in this collection were published previously. Some of them have been altered significantly since their original publication and may have been published under different titles.

"Bleeding the Sky" has appeared on Sappho's Torque.

"Commonly Occurring in Villages, in Hamlets, and on Hearths Around Our Great Land" first appeared in *Curbside Review*.

"Floodtide: My Unhiding" has appeared on the Poetry Super Highway and in PHUI e-magazine.

"Listening for Atlantis" has appeared on the Poetry Super Highway and in *Falcon Wings 2001*.

"Long-Distance" first appeared in *Best Poems of 1997*.

"Moving to Your Home" has appeared in the *Houston Poetry Fest Anthology 1999*, in PHUI e-magazine, and on the Poetry Super Highway.

"New Love in Dead Cornfields" has appeared in the *Educators' Poetry Anthology 2002* and in *Falcon Wings 2001*.

"The Path Often Traveled, the Path Less Celebrated, the Path of Ennobled Resistance (A Rule-Breaking Poem for a Nail-Biting Vigil)" first appeared in *Yellow Chair Review* on November 10, 2016.

"The Wilderness of Waters" first appeared in PHUI e-magazine.

poems which previously appeared in the chapbook *Gypsies*:
- After
- Book with Forgotten Title
- Cleaning House
- Good-Night
- His Ballad at Breakfast
- Joan and the City
- Joyride
- Long-Distance
- Los Angeles
- Lullaby for a Crying Child
- Manifest Destiny
- Moving Out
- The Usual

poems which previously appeared in the chapbook *Barefoot on Marble*:
- Barefoot on Marble Fragments
- Bleeding the Sky
- Commonly Occurring in Villages, in Hamlets, and on Hearths Around Our Great Land
- Floodtide: My Unhiding
- Half-Truths Inside Villanelle
- Listening for Atlantis
- Moving to Your Home
- New Love in Dead Cornfields

- Ruby / Renew / Redux
- Summer Night Rite
- The Awakening of Jack Brown
- The Hummingbirds Warned
- The Modern Woman's Guide to Modern Life
- The Wilderness of Waters
- Wedding List Poem

Hello!

I hope you enjoyed reading *The Sharp Edges of Water*. There is no greater honor for me as a writer than to know that a reader has appreciated my work. And if this collection of poems has left you with a good impression, it would be wonderful karma for you to tell others about it and to share your enjoyment of it on social media.

There is also no greater support you can give an author than your word-of-mouth recommendation, so please do share your enthusiasm! It would mean so much to me if you would leave a review for *The Sharp Edges of Water* on any book review site or on your book blog.

Thank you!

Index of First Lines

countdown calendar of what to do and when................76
Do not go gentle into that stifling night.....................83
Down this deep, debate over waves..........................28
Fourteen cows piled themselves onto the
    New Jersey turnpike......................................74
Golden ball like a prophet.......................................65
He remembers her hair...37
His was one firm hand that grabbed at nothing............41
I cannot tell you...42
I remember a princess..26
I see you, my gray wool sweater...............................32
I wait behind the closed chapel doors,
    hanging on my...73
I was a roller skating queen.....................................66
I wash your letters..57
in a throbbing fog, I walk the hall.............................58
In the time when my fingernails...............................52
In your room with the fireplace, still.........................34
It has been made quite clear that the world.................81
languish under dust like the palest sheets....................59
Little bird..84
lizards crawl all over...67
Los Angeles isn't flat...22
Memories quicken my pulse....................................55
midnight here, two in the.......................................49
my room...19
O Los Angeles, your grumbling................................20

O painted, sun-glinting......................................30
She stood, chained to...44
small sweet pieces of time crumbling away...................54
Ten hummingbirds sat buzzing, hovering.....................50
The engine cries...24
The long and lonely road stretches............................35
There was a cape, cold and wet and worn,
   that he said had..79
There was fear..61
There was no expression in his eyes...........................51
We've been sitting on the bed.................................71
When my cousin died, olive skin and thick...................69
Your ocean here is warm and green...........................70

Ways to Support Authors

*There are many ways to support an author
whose work you admire!*

Request their book at your local library.
Review their book on any and all bookselling and book review sites.
Follow the author on social media and share their posts.
Take a selfie with their book and share it on social media.
Attend the author's events.
Suggest their book for your book club.
Recommend the author as a speaker or workshop leader.
Tell your friends about the book.
Include the book in a blog post or list of your favorites.
Nominate their book for an award.
Ask your local bookstore to stock the book.
Support the author's other projects, including pre-ordering their next book.
Add a copy of their book to your local Little Free Library.
Buy their book as a gift for someone.

Authors everywhere thank you!

About the Author

Photo credit Lauren Volness.

Angélique Jamail's poetry and essays have appeared in over two dozen anthologies and journals, including New Reader Magazine, Waxwing, *Time-Slice*, *Improbable Worlds*, Pluck Magazine, *The Milk of Female Kindness — An Anthology of Honest Motherhood*, *Untameable City: Poems on the Nature of Houston*, Femmeliterate, Bayou City Magazine, and *The Enchantment of the Ordinary*. Her magic realism novelette *Finis.* (Odeon Press) has been praised by fiction writer Ari Marmell as having "some of the most real people I've encountered via text in a long time," and by poet Marie Marshall as "a witty tale of conformity, prejudice, and transformation, in a world that is disturbing as much for its familiarity as for its strangeness."

She teaches English and Creative Writing to high school students. She resides in the Houston area with her family and a couple of cats who have their own gravity. She has otherwise lived in her imagination pretty much her whole life.

Read more of her work, and find out about upcoming publications, on her blog Sappho's Torque and her website. Also find her in the realm of social media on Facebook and Twitter. She's available for book club appearances in person or via Skype.

www.SapphosTorque.com
www.AngeliqueJamail.com
Twitter: @AngeliqueJamail

www.ingramcontent.com/pod-product-compliance
Lightning Source LLC
Chambersburg PA
CBHW030236100526
44584CB00015BB/1501